MUSLIMS IN FRANCE

The way towards
coexistence

TARIQ RAMADAN

THE ISLAMIC FOUNDATION

Published by
The Islamic Foundation, Markfield Conference Centre,
Ratby Lane, Markfield, Leicester LE67 9SY, United Kingdom
Tel: (01530) 244944, Fax: (01530) 244946
E-mail: i.foundation@islamic-foundation.org.uk
Web site: http://www.islamic-foundation.org.uk/islamfound

Quran House, PO Box 30611, Nairobi, Kenya

PMB 3193, Kano, Nigeria

ISBN 0 86037 299 5 (PB)

Contents

Preface

The Muslim presence in France dates back to the Middle Ages, during the time of the Andalusian epoch. Muslims lived then mostly in the south of the country, particularly in Avignon. Decades elapsed before the arrival of new waves of Muslims at the beginning of the 20th century, between the two World Wars, and particularly after 1945. The latter arrived in their tens of thousands, chiefly from Algeria but also from Morocco and Tunisia, to work mainly in factories and on building sites. France, in full social and economic reconstruction after a devastating war, needed labourers. The immigration policy, until the 1960s, was somewhat chaotic and the agreements made with the governments of the South (such as Algeria in 1964) were not strictly applied. During almost two decades the waves of immigration did not cease and this has produced an exponential increase of North African immigrants: from 48,000 in 1964 the Algerians numbered 160,000 in 1973; in the same period the number of Moroccans increased from 50,000 to 400,000.[1] It was not until the 1970s, during the economic crisis, that the French government started toughening its immigration policy, bringing in strict laws regarding entry to French territories. A policy of repatriation was even elaborated in 1977: immigrants were offered subsidies to help them to return to Algeria, Morocco or Tunisia. However, this enterprise met with little success and the number of immigrants, though in a less dramatic fashion, kept increasing, mainly owing to two reasons. This was due, on the one hand, to familial regrouping with the arrival in France of the workers' wives and children; and on the other hand, to clandestine immigration, which increased upon the application of the more restrictive immigration laws. In the 1980s the situation stabilised a little, and

5

by the end of that decade it became clear that the second, and with it the third and fourth, generations had taken root, and that for the great majority of them, France had become their country.

The number of Muslims in France has been the object of the most diverse estimations. If their presence is evaluated at around 3 million by official census, other statistics suggest 4 and, very often, 5 million. Evaluations vary, but it is reasonable to consider that a figure of 4 million has been reached and, without much doubt, slightly exceeded. Half of the Muslims living in France hold, therefore, French nationality and this, very explicitly, makes Islam a reality within the French landscape. It is now the second largest religion in France.

Despite the objective nature of these facts, many intellectuals and social and political players continue to think of and present Islam as an exogenous fact that is closely linked to immigration, and particularly to clandestine immigration. This is either a question of a poor knowledge of reality or, more strategically, of a discourse entertained for electoral ends in an epoch that sees racism and xenophobia once again on the increase. Nonetheless, even if, in certain respects, the problems are linked, it is clear today that the question of Islam in France has nothing to do with the inextricable difficulties of unemployment or immigration.

The extreme right party of Jean-Marie le Pen entertains the fear of an "Arab-Muslim" invasion and the loss of French identity by nourishing a discourse that is intentionally confusing regarding "foreigners", unemployment, clandestine immigration and Islam. The first Muslims arrived in France in a perfectly legal manner (often at the request of employers) and their children have also become legal French citizens. Whilst the serious question of clandestine immigration must be resolved, this must be distinguished from the Islamic reality in France, just as, from now on, the Muslims, whether resident or French citizens, should be considered the victims of unemployment rather than its cause. (See Fig.1.)

The 1990s has witnessed the appearance, after the "Islamic scarf" affair of the young schoolgirls in 1989, of a new kind of questioning about Islam. The "visibility" of the youth who are coming back to

Rate of Unemployment According to Nationality from 1980 to 1990

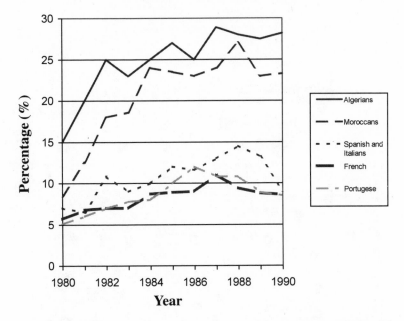

Fig. I. Based on: P. Bernard, *"L'Immigration"*, (Le Monde Poche, 1993) p.98

practising their religion, the increasing number of places for Prayers in cellars and basements, and the demand for *ḥalāl* meat is a phenomena that has led intellectuals to question the compatibility of Islam with a secularised society. For their part, Muslims have passed through a normal stage of transition which, as we shall see, will have a decisive influence on the future.

Note

I.   See Jørgen Nielsen, *Muslims in Western Europe* (Edinburgh University Press, 1995), pp. 8–9.

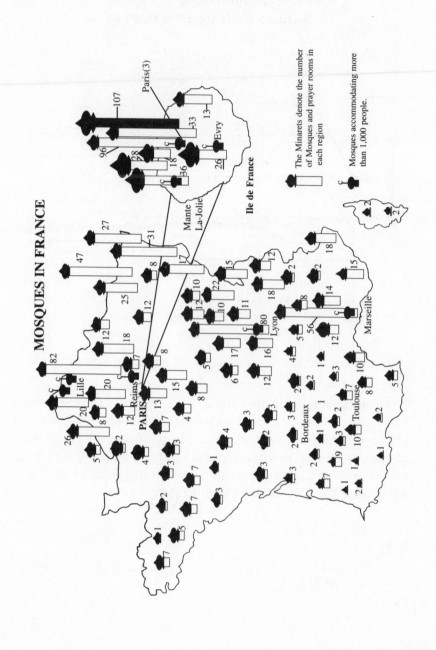

MOSQUES IN FRANCE

The Minarets denote the number of Mosques and prayer rooms in each region

Mosques accommodating more than 1,000 people.

Paris(3)

Ile de France

Mante La-Jolie

Lille

Reims

PARIS

Lyon

Bordeaux

Toulouse

Marseille

Evry

Introduction

France is experiencing difficult times. Many social and economic problems are surfacing and the situation is becoming more complicated by the day. It is a known fact that one of the major social problems in France now is the state of affairs in those suburbs bordering the big cities such as Paris, Lyon and Marseille. In such cities, the young generation, particularly among the immigrant population (Algerian, Tunisian, Moroccan), present a serious issue for the French government and the local authorities. They do not know how to manage this deep social crisis. Marginality, juvenile delinquency and increasing poverty have created a volatile situation. Over the course of the last 15 years, yet another phenomena, the *"return to Islam"*, is visible at the level of social classes, especially among the North African youth. Associations and groups are being formed everywhere and the leaders of these various tendencies try to answer the needs of their communities. Despite the many, and incessant, divisions between these associations, the movement as a whole is increasing by means of youth affiliation, and the latter are proud of their new-found religious and cultural identity. The French government views this development unfavourably and is suspicious both at home and abroad. This new trend is considered a danger to French political interests. Recently, the Home Minister stated that "delinquency" is "more preferable in France" than "fundamentalism" (*intégrisme*), thereby tainting all active groups in French society.

Such a statement, expressed by one of the most important ministers of State, reflects the French government's attitude towards this "very sensitive subject". A whole host of reasons could be cited and may have led to this situation; for example, France's colonial past and the steady increase in and the visible presence of "foreigners". The political discourse, as well as the indigenous communities' response to the presence of Muslims in France is based more upon emotional outbursts and less on well-thought-out arguments and analyses. The same phenomena is noticed in the Muslim community. Among the youth, marginalised and unemployed, we are witnessing a tendency towards confinement, rejection and radicalisation. The leaders of the various Muslim associations and organisations seem to fall into the same trap and often take some extreme position. Therefore, positive encounters are few and far between as is dialogue and coexistence.

Such a treatment reveals serious deficiencies and could have deplorable consequences, if Muslims confine themselves to its conclusions. Firstly, it prevents them from having a clear vision of historical developments and more recent advancements within French society. Secondly, Muslims in France are increasingly realising their inadequacies to analyse and reflect upon the reality of the French Constitution, its laws and its wider implications. Beyond the passionate debates and the mutual rejections, Muslims have to bring their minds to bear on the fact that it is the frame of the French legislation which has to be, at this stage, their frame of reference also. A deeper analysis shows that the room for manoeuvre as far as coexistence is conceived, within the legal framework is very wide, and offers a number of possibilities for Muslims in France to avail. Total mastery of these objective data (i.e. the Constitution, laws, etc.) is required in order to solve the major problems facing the Muslim community. This must also be the principal ground for discussion with the French authorities.

Very few Muslim scholars are engaged in this important and urgent task of exploring the constitutional and legal issues in the country. The field is thus left open to non-Muslim French sociologists, political scientists, lawyers and others who usually present a great many studies and researches, with elements of both good and bad, to their readers. These studies, however, are received by their French compatriots as the only and possible interpretation of Muslim society. Furthermore, the hopes and aspirations of Muslims and their views are trivialised by some who are increasingly seen as authorities on Muslim issues.[1] The Muslims lack credible researches, and hence informed opinions and imaginative directions for the community which could provide much needed influence in the social and political spheres of the country.

Though it is important for Muslims to reflect upon the constitutional and legal aspects, one cannot ignore however, the inherited images of Islam and Arabs in the French psyche.[2] Images of "dirty", "fanatic" and "violent" Muslims are widespread among average French men and women. Old medieval prejudices and biases regarding the "world of Islam" are simply carried over and disseminated by the media under a variety of names and slogans. This fear is further compounded by the scars of the Algerian War of Liberation, 1954–62. In spite of technological progress, which has reduced distances and facilitated communications, erroneous images of Islam and Muslims remain the rule.

The second part of this study will focus on the principal areas of misunderstanding between the Muslims and the indigenous French people and will analyse the major shifts in the Muslim posture and activities over the last ten years in France. This will offer us a general framework within which we have to consider the future stakes of coexistence such as the representation and implementation of Islam (Islamic education, *da'wa*, etc.).

Notes

1. For example, Gilles Kepel's *A l'Ouest d'Allah* (Editions du Seuil, Paris, 1994) presented as academic research, is a popular book written in a journalistic style with countless anecdotes. Its impact on the average reader is, in this way, sizable in spite of its inaccuracies, gaps and errors.

2. On this specific subject, see the illuminating article "Islam and the Construction of Europe" by Roger Ballard, in *Muslims in the Margin: Political Responses to the Presence of Islam in Western Europe* (Pharos, Den Haag, 1996), pp. 15–51. Ballard develops an interesting argument where he explains the age-old view of "the Muslim" as the prototype of the "alien" (which was initiated, according to him, by the dualistic theological thought of Saint Augustine).

PART I

Part I

The Present Situation

A. Historical Elements

The presence of Muslims in France, with all the problems it has involved at different levels (religious, social, cultural and political), has spurred a number of historians and religious representatives (particularly, of course, Jews, Catholics and Protestants) to study their own history with the intention of reassessing and reconsidering the foundations of French secularism. Since 1989, the number of articles, researches, and books on this issue has increased considerably. The first "scarf affair",[1] which pruned the issue of the "integration" of Muslims, seems to have challenged the essence of the French Constitution, which was conceived and written a long time before Muslim settlement in France. In their studies, some try to demonstrate that the framework of the Constitution is indisputable and that Muslims have to subscribe to it totally. Others discuss the evolution and development of laws over the last 300 years and particularly since 1905, the year when the State and Church were constitutionally separated. They point out that the Constitution could be seen as a growing and evolving mechanism which maintained the freedom and equality of French society and, therefore, French Muslims' needs and aspirations could be incorporated into the French legal system. Professor Jean Baubérot is a protagonist of such a view. His opinions are well known in France through his numerous publications on religion and secularism. In his book, *La Laïcité, quel Héritage?*,[2] he emphasises the two stages of French secularisation: from the Medieval period up to the French Revolution (1789). This was when the people of France struggled to free themselves from the yoke of the suppressive "Medieval Regime" (*L'Ancien Régime*), from its oppressive social order, and from the Church which supported it. The effect of this liberation process was the legal recognition of other religions and the freedom of worship (for both Protestants and Jews). In 1789, it was acknowledged that a "non-Catholic can elect and be elected",[3] but with a restriction concerning the Jews who still were not considered as "full citizens". The *Universal Declaration of Human and Citizen Rights* (1791), in its Tenth Article states, clearly, that no one can be constrained or persecuted because of his beliefs, religion or colour. The first stage of an official and social recognition of religious pluralism was thus in place.

During the 19th century, conflicts between the advocates of secularism, the rationalists and the so-called "free-thinkers" on the one hand, and the Pope and the Roman Church on the other, never stopped. These tense relations perpetuated themselves until the beginning of this century. Inevitably, they left scars and resentment on both sides. It was in this fraught atmosphere that the second stage of secularisation, according to Baubérot, was achieved, though the Constitution explicitly fixed the legal framework within which private affairs, hitherto linked with religion, were henceforth separated from public policy. This question remained sensitive, emotional and passionate.[4]

During the 1870s, the conflict focused on education. Minister Jules Ferry intervened in the debate, bringing to bear an important influence in the adoption of several laws which fixed the *laïque* frame of the French Constitution[5] throughout the last 20 years of the 19th century (not only in the field of education but also concerning the legal permission for divorce, burial, medical organisation, freedom of the press and so on). The process speeded up and on the 11th December 1905 the Law of separation between the Church and the State was promulgated; henceforth, the State was to protect freedom of conscience and worship but would not recognise any specific cult. Therefore, religion was to be a free and private affair and the State was to function as a neutral guardian of the public administration and was not to provide remuneration or any kind of subsidies to priests. The adoption of this Law, after almost a century of conflict, was obviously perceived as a victory for the advocates of "genuine secularism", which was often similar to an "anti-clerical" or "anti-religious" attitude. This was, in fact, the interpretation of the Church which, a year earlier (1904), had broken off its diplomatic relations with the French State, thereby demonstrating the total disagreement between the Church and the Republic.

This long history, made up of bitter fights, conflicts and mutual rejections, finally gave specific identity to the French Republic. In the minds of many politicians and scholars, its secular characteristic is the essential feature which distinguishes France from all other countries in Europe as well as from America.[6] This perception, in fact, is not ill-founded and a close study of the history and formulation of the French Constitution shows that the nature of the French separation between religion and public life, is actually different from that of other European countries. Yet, this objective statement is not sufficient to explain the reasons for the deep tension we observe in France today; incidentally, it is not strictly a question of *laïcité* and its legal system.

B.   What Does the Law Say?

The Law of 11th December 1905 is still in force and it is referred to in all debates concerning French secularism. Without going into an exhaustive analysis of the complexities of this law – as such a study would be beyond the scope of this work – we can, here, bring to the fore three major principles which follow from its enforcement:

1.   The State is neutral and recognises all religions. Its neutrality demands that it must remain *equidistant* from all religions without interfering in any religious affair: such as in theology, representation, the choice of priest (for example *Rabbi* or *Imām*), subsidies, etc.[7] In this sense *neutrality* clearly means *equality* or, in more precise words, *"a means to protect the equality of treatment of all religions facing the law"*. By extension, the neutrality of State employees is required, and this is a logical consequence of the State's function as a whole.[8]

2.   Religion is a personal and private affair and the State has to assure and protect total freedom of worship. In this sense, State neutrality is also a kind of *recognition*[9] which implies that the State should provide for each religion, on an equal footing, the means to worship and its contingent obligations. There is no

question of interfering in religious affairs, as we have already mentioned above, but of granting and furnishing religions as equal, providing for their needs (for example, building sites and other similar facilities).[10]

3. As a consequence of the State's neutrality, the official recognition of all religions, and the legal protection of the freedom of worship, the Government has, not only to respect, but also to protect *the total independence* of the Muslims of France. This independence essentially means the right for Muslims to determine what is the priority in their practise of Islam,[11] to organise themselves as well as to fix the curricula of their private Islamic education (in mosques, Islamic centres, etc.), and to decide what should be the nature of their representative structure (Committee of coordination, elected Council, Federation, etc.).

One of the important principles of French secularism, known as "The Republic Unity" (*"l'Unité de la République"*), is based on the three dimensions – or consequences – of the Law of 1905: namely, state neutrality, the recognition and independence of the Muslims. To complete the picture, we have to add that the secular state, which wants to defend the "Republic Unity", even if it recognises religion as a fact and Muslims as citizens or foreign residents, does not however consider the idea of a "Muslim community". In the eyes of the law such a concept is devoid of any meaning: integration has to be *individual* and any acceptance of the notion of community would lead to social divisions and fractures within French society. Individual integration is the only means, in the minds of many French politicians and academics, that will guarantee strict respect of the equality of people facing the laws and safeguard a genuine religious pluralism.[12] "Muslims must know and respect the French legal frame", said Jean-Claude Barreau the adviser to Charles Pasqua, the former Minister of Home Affairs, "because it partakes of the French identity: neither them nor any other religions are empowered to call into question its foundations".[13] Therefore, it is necessary to consider closely the implications of this "French legal frame" concerning Muslims *in/of* France.[14]

C. Concrete Corollaries

Problems concerning the Muslim's presence in France seem merely to stem from two directions. On the one hand, Muslims are not aware of the content, scope and even consequences of the law, and, on the other, French politicians or academics have an elementary knowledge of Islam as a religion and way of life (when these elements are not widespread erroneous biases and prejudices).[15]

Despite all passionate debates and mutual misunderstandings, the Constitution offers to Muslims an important element of manoeuvrability to fulfil their religious obligations. Laws, however, are not the chief problem today: the State Council, for instance, as we have seen above, has stated that wearing the scarf is not in contradiction with the Constitution. This is one example among many others: it would appear then, that French laws are less on edge concerning Islam than are French politicians.[16] It is possible to bring to the fore at least five rights from which Muslims could benefit today all of which are contained within the French Constitutional framework:

(a) *Right to knowledge*: the whole population enjoys this right. For Muslims, according to one of the most important principles of their religion, to have access to knowledge is imperative. In France, as in a majority of European countries, the legal principle of "compulsory education" for all children offers Muslims the means to apply the famous *ḥadīth*: "Seeking knowledge is a duty for all Muslims (male and female)."[17] Muslims have to acknowledge that fellow Muslims do not have this right even in a majority Muslim country where illiteracy rates sometimes reach 70%.[18]

(b) *Right to practice Islam*: today, Muslims living in France can observe the major Islamic practices. There is no ban on praying, paying *zakāt*, fasting or going on Pilgrimage to Makka. In several cities there may be some administrative problems in building mosques as we have stated earlier but, in general, basic needs are provided for. Debates concerning the scarf (*ḥijāb*), Muslim cemeteries and *ḥalāl* meat are particularly intense and are symptomatic of the tense and nervous climate in society, but they should not lead us to omit what is actually acquired concerning day-to-day practice. Once more, neither the scarf nor Muslim sections in cemeteries relate to real legal problems and the turbulence they bring about in public life is due to the fact that they affect the sensitive and more global question of French identity, today and in the future. What is it? What will this identity be if French society has to integrate, and so identify itself in, these new behaviours and buildings, which are so strange and so *visible*?[19] All this does not affect the application of the principle of freedom of worship; if the rate of daily practise is so low (between 15 and 20% of the total Muslim population),[20] it is not due to some kind of government restriction or pressure but rather for reasons internal to the Muslim community itself.[21]

(c)   *Right to form an Association*: according to the law, Muslims, as any other people living in France, have the right to form an association. In this respect, two Articles of the French Constitution are commonly referred to: the Law of 1901, which concerns all associations interested in social affairs in general, such as culture, the arts or sports. The Law of 1905, which determines the secular character of the French State, also incorporates (Chapter IV) the "freedom of religious association within the framework of the law of association of 1 July 1901".[22] Associations formed between 1939 and 1981, were bound by law to be registered with the authorities and they were "subject to the approval of the Ministry of the Interior".[23] On 9th October 1981, this restriction was lifted and ever since every group has been allowed to set up an association, without any legal approval from the authorities. Thanks to this, the number of Muslim associations in France has risen considerably during the last 15 years. Now there are approximately 1,400 of them.[24] Each one works independently without interference from the authorities. However, at times government bodies and authorities prefer one over and above another.

(d)   *Right to autonomous representation*: nothing within the French Constitution prevents Muslims from organising themselves either at local or at national level. They are totally free to set up the structures they think most appropriate for themselves. We pointed out earlier various successive French government's interference in Muslim organisations and it is obvious that to find a common basis for unity among Muslims remains a far cry from the truth. This results from the Muslims' inability to lay down a common framework for an independent council that could educate Muslims and negotiate with the government on their behalf. There are more than eight national associations or federations claiming to represent Muslims struggling to find a common framework.[25] It is important to remember here that, legally speaking, there are no obstacles for Muslims to go further in organising themselves.

(e) *Right to appeal*: in all affairs concerning religious, administrative or legal problems Muslims have the right, like any other member of society to appeal to a court of law to seek a fair trial against a decision seemingly ill-founded or unfair. The "State of Law" (*"l'Etat de Droit"*) is not perfect, of course, nonetheless it offers important guarantees to protect individual or organisational rights.[26] As we have pointed out earlier, the consulting opinion of the French "State Council" regarding the scarf issue has established a precedent for courts all over the country. In some cases, where Muslim girls won their cases to wear *ḥijāb* in schools, the courts even decided to compensate them.[27] Muslims have this right as do all other citizens. Obviously, the problem is not a legal deficiency regarding the rights of Muslims in France, rather the problem clearly lies in their ignorance as well as negligence of legal matters. Muslims do not have this opportunity both at individual as well as at collective level. Only in the last few years have Muslims in France approached the courts to defend their rights. Thus they have gradually become aware of the judicial system and its benefits. They are realising that, in some way, redressing their grievances through the judicial system avoids a passionate debate about Islam which is often based on prejudices or international considerations which interfere in an objective assessment of the facts. The law has to protect the integrity and rights of each citizen or resident in the light of events. Justice, very often, has been done in the Muslims' favour. The Muslims, therefore, have to learn how the judicial system works and then proceed.

These five "fundamental rights" are available today and certainly Muslims can benefit from them. Within this current French legal system, Muslims are quite "free" to act and this is important. Objectively and legally speaking, the French secular system is not as closed as it appears unless we only consider its narrow interpretation by those who are afraid of a too *visible and active* Muslim presence.[28] These latter speak about "Muslim integration" in a restrictive sense and refer to the concept of "integration" in contrast with two other patterns, namely "assimilation" and "isolation".[29] According to them, there is a social philosophy within the principle of "*l'Unité de la République*" that France has to protect and preserve as one of its most important features. Therein, the Muslim presence is not merely a strict question of the law.

D. Three Patterns

The problem of minorities is complex and particularly difficult to apprehend and, consequently, to solve. It has been, for a long time, a preoccupation of lawyers and it has become still more strenuous with the building of the European Community[30] and the collapse of the communist model in the East European countries since 1989. So how to deal with emerging nationalist, ethnic or religious claims? How to construct unity through all these differences and incessant appeals to secession heard throughout Europe? This problem is of the highest importance and it may be one of the weightiest challenges European countries are going to face in the near future. In this landscape, the Muslim presence within each West European country adds a new and perilous problem: if immigrant people of the first generation have been considered as "foreigners", is this not the case with second, third, or fourth generation Muslims? In France, for instance, youths of North African origin are French in a large majority. They are French, but they are French and Muslim: they are from *here*, they are *at home*, but with a religion and a culture from *there,* "unfamiliar" to the French people, strange and *foreign*. With this duality of the young Muslims in France, the question becomes, then, how to preserve the famous "Republic Unity"? What is the legal framework that can safeguard both national unity and religious-cultural identity?

Academics in general and sociologists in particular have fixed three patterns which are supposed to explain all the possibilities as to the type of minority presence in Western countries:

1. *Assimilation*: the assimilationist view supposes a total amalgamation between the immigrant and the new cultural way of living which welcomes him/her. He/she is asked to "forget" his/her references or culture and opt for a total and complete merger with the host community culture. These were the attempts made during the first wave of immigration (between the end of the Second World War and the 1970s). The same treatment was offered to Italians, Portuguese, Spaniards and Arabs (Muslims in majority): the French authorities thought then, without giving much consideration to differences of culture, that assimilation would similarly have a positive influence on those peoples. They tried, for about 30 years, to disregard religious and cultural particularities. Hitherto, this naïve conception has been universally recognised as an error and few people today believe in the notion of "assimilation" as a way towards positive coexistence.

2. *Isolation*: is exactly the opposite to the assimilationist position. The isolationist believes in the preservation of the immigrants' religious and cultural beliefs and practices. However, this provokes separations and divisions in society and encourages ghettos and ghetto mentalities. Relations between ethnic or religious groups are quite non-existent and notions of the nation's unity are discouraged; consequently, the idea of "Republic" becomes meaningless.

As we mentioned earlier, this model, for the majority of French politicians and academics, is an "anti-model", one which is associated with Anglo-Saxon social organisation and policy. According to them, it is exactly what France should avoid if it wants to preserve the principle of "Republic Unity".[31]

3. *Integration*: the concept of integration has been fashionable in France since the mid-1980s when the *SOS Racism* movement made it its slogan: "Integration, it works! Integration, it is possible" (*"L'intégration, ça marche! L'intégration, c'est possible"*). This approach was created and sustained by media pundits and politicians like Bernard-Henry Levy and Julien Dray. This popular movement enjoyed considerable influence among the young immigrants of the second generation (called *les beurs et les beurettes*) until the beginning of the 1990s. Now, the slogan is losing its claim. Its main objective was to fight increasing and visible racism in France, particularly in

certain regions such as Lyon, Marseilles and Paris where the percentage of immigrants was highest and coexistence most difficult. According to the leaders and scholars of this movement, "integration" means to admit that all these youths, with their skin colour, origin, culture, and religion, are French and have the same rights as any indigenous French person. From now on, they partake of this "new France" with its multicultural landscape: they must be respected and protected in their individuality, their particularities and their rights from the moment they themselves respect the French Republic's fundamental principles and values.

Equidistant from "assimilation" and "isolation", "integration", to which academics and politicians have been referring hitherto, seems to be the "middle path" in the way that the State recognises and respects the individual in his or her cultural or religious characteristics but the latter, beforehand, has to swear allegiance to the French Constitution and its principles of secularism (*laïcité*) and "Republic Unity". There is a need to find the right balance between individual identity and the requirements of social unity that make possible a harmonious coexistence. This theoretical tolerance has not yet materialised and the "scarf affair" reveals the depth of the problem of the Muslim presence, and its visibility, in France today. To say that the State has to recognise and respect the religious identity of everyone supposes, for instance, that the French State and Muslims are in agreement on what exactly constitutes a Muslim's identity. Are the wearing of a scarf, the construction of mosques and the demands for Muslim cemeteries from the State, the eating of *ḥalāl* meat, counted as *Islamic* or Muslim needs or is there an implicit expression of "fundamentalism" or "fanaticism"? Who will judge? From whom can we expect a fair judgement to be delivered? The French State has chosen interlocutors, such as the Rector of the Paris Mosque, and seems to have decided this unilaterally, no consultation has taken place. So, even the theoretical principle of the balance of mutual respect and recognition seems to have been abandoned. This despite the fact that the former Interior Minister, Charles Pasqua, and his adviser proclaim that France is "the most tolerant country in Europe".[32]

In Switzerland, as in Germany or the UK, the concept of "integration" as understood by the French State has certain similarities with the "assimilationist" pattern. Under the same appellation of "integration", practices (such as scarves, cemeteries, meat, etc.) are respected in Switzerland, Belgium or Germany in the name of freedom of conscience and worship but are considered in France as expressions of extremism and fanaticism. The concept of *integration* is very wide in European countries: however, constant reference to it is not enough to explain the tensions which underlie French society.

French history is one of a permanent conflict between the State and the Roman Holy See. More than it being a single problem with the Islamic religion, French culture and secular tradition have a historical contention with "religion" as a fact and particularly with its visible presence. This does not mean that religion is not present or does not play an important role within society – at least as a cultural reference – but this means, implicitly, that religious leaders and institutions have had to learn, over the last two centuries, to be very discreet and unobtrusive. They play an important part, but behind both public and political scenes. The recent arrival of the "Islamic problem" in France has thrown this tacit agreement back into question, i.e. the distribution of functions between the political and religious spheres. First of all, the Islamic practice is *visible*, especially concerning dress – the number of women wearing scarves in France has been increasing year by year. Today, the demand for mosques, cemeteries and respect for Islamic dietary laws pushes Muslims to found organisations which interfere in the social scene in the name of their religion and in doing so they develop a new feeling of community belonging, which is seemingly far from the adherence to the principle of "Unity of the Republic". Islam appears to disturb the rules of the game: what kind of integration could be proposed in such circumstances?

In a recent book, Jocelyn Cesari describes a "new secular pact" (*pour un nouveau pacte laïque*)[33] which, she believes, should take into account the new Muslim presence and allow them to find their place in French society. Many Muslim organisations have appealed, during the last seven years, for a reassessment of the idea of secularism: they declare that they recognise and accept its global frame (which should permit a balanced integration) but that it has to be read in the light of the new reality of French society with its new Muslim component.[34] Limited legal reform could be introduced, or at least discussed, to permit a respect of both French identity and Muslim worship: when all is said and done, it appears that it is more a question of strictly implementing what the laws say rather than a matter of reform. If only Muslims in France knew – or were interested in – these laws and tried to organise themselves in order to obtain the rights which are effectively theirs. This is, maybe, one of the important keys regarding the current problem of coexistence.

Notes

1. In 1989, three young Moroccan girls were expelled from their school because they wore the "Islamic scarf" (ḥijāb). It soon became a State affair within which Hassan II, the Moroccan King, also became involved (he asked the girls to remove the ḥijāb).

2. See Jean Baubérot, La Laïcité, quel Héritage? (Secularism, Which Heritage?), (Labor et Fides, Paris, 1990).

3. See Tariq Ramadan, Les Musulmans dans la Laïcité (Tawḥīd, Lyon, 1994), pp. 28–30.

4. Muslims have to bear this point in mind: French society does not have a problem with "Islam and Muslims" per se; it has, rather, a historical contention with "religion" as a whole. Some reactions in the French audience cannot be understood without considering this point; this will help us to go beyond the simplistic, but widespread, idea that Muslims are the only "victims" of the "hatred" of French racism and its rejection of Islam.

5. Especially the famous Law adopted on 28th March 1882, which makes primary school compulsory and laïque. The expression "moral and religious education" was substituted for "moral and civic education".

6. In a French TV programme, on 13th October 1994 (La Marche du Siècle), Jean-Claude Barreau, adviser to the Minister of Foreign Affairs (Charles Pasqua), was asked about the scarf affair. He answered emphatically that: "France is not like the other European countries; France is the most tolerant nation thanks to its specific secularism and all the other countries have to take it as an example."

7. Many Muslims recalled this fact when the Interior Minister Pierre Joxe established, in 1989, the CORIF (Conseil de Réflexion sur l'Islam en France) which was supposed to be "an interlocutor with public powers". They argue that this consulting structure is not representative of the Muslims in France and that only Muslims have the ability to decide for themselves who is able to speak on their behalf. See Catherine Withol de Wenden, "Muslims in France", in W.A.R. Shadid and P.S. Van Koningsveld (eds.), Muslims in the Margin: Political Responses to the Presence of Islam in Western Europe (Pharos, Den Haag, 1996), p. 58. The author rightly explains: "This

consultation structure of nine wise men, which was not really representative of all the trends of Islam, has not been consulted by Charles Pasqua since 1993 and the Head of the Great Mosque of Paris, Dalil Boubakeur, has given birth to a new structure in November 1993, the *Conseil Représentatif des Musulmans de France.*" This new structure, with its Charter, published in January 1995, suffered similar deficiencies. In a recent article, Milton Viorst puts forward the following sound comment: "Not surprisingly, the Charter also named the Paris Mosque the official spokesman for the community. For most Muslims, this confirmed that the document was written on Pasqua's typewriter. To Pasqua's chagrin, most Muslim leaders proceeded to turn their back on the Charter, leaving the government with one more useless document on its growing stack of failures to organise the Muslims of France." See "The Muslims of France", *Foreign Affairs,* Washington, DC (September/ October 1996). This allegation was confirmed when the well-known French scholar, Bruno Etienne, openly said that he was involved in the writing of this Charter after he had been requested by the French Interior Minister's cabinet. All these vain attempts are contrary to the principles of French law.

8. The French "State Council" (the State consultative juridical organ empowered to give opinions concerning legal decisions or the adequacy of a law with the Constitution) reminded the Government of this principle when it was consulted about the "veil" of the three young Muslim girls expelled from their school in 1989. Neutrality is requested from State employees, not from "users of State services"; so, says the State Council, the wearing of the scarf is not in contradiction with the French Constitution.

9. In the text of the Law of 1905, the term "recognition" disappeared to avoid confusion with the kind of "official recognition" which had been enforced until then. Still, it remains a "recognition of the religious institutions" the difference being that the State does not finance any religion.

10. Many Muslims complain that this rule is not equally enforced. In a number of cities, Muslim associations face resistance and clear opposition from the local administration to Mosque building projects. In reality, such requests are translated into a complex administrative process which demands a long time and an incredible amount of paper work. It often happens that the local Mayors buy the site (or encourage other associations to buy it) during the acquisition process initiated by Muslim associations. Many studies report this disparity of treatment. See Gilles Kepel, *Les Banlieues de l'Islam, Naissance d'une Religion en France* (Editions du Seuil, Paris, 1987); and Jocelyn Cesari, *Etre Musulman en France* (Karthala, Paris, 1994).

11. That means to answer the question: "What is Islam?" or, more precisely, "What must a Muslim do if he or she wants to correctly practise his or her religion in France?"

12. A bad example of integration would be, in the minds of such politicians and researchers, the Anglo-Saxon model of social organisation which has produced "cultural and religious ghettos". Without entering, here, into an argument about the validity of such an assertion, we could note that the

immigration of workers during the 1970s, has in fact created many ghettos in France itself. North African immigrants have been "parked" in estates, away from large cities. Its consequences today are the suburban crises with the growth of marginality, unemployment, delinquency and poverty, chiefly among immigrant populations. This perhaps is the main cause of the present growth of racism in France. In a recent survey, more than 70% of the French populace said they agreed with some of Jean-Marie le Pen's ideas, the leader of the far right party, "*Le Front National*".

13. In the TV programme "*La Marche du Siècle*", 13th October 1994.

14. Charles Pasqua, in his speech during the inauguration of Lyon's largest Mosque (April 1994), affirmed that henceforth we must not use the expression "Islam *in* France" ("*L'islam en France*") but rather speak about the "Islam *of* France" ("*L'islam de France*"). The choice of the preposition "*of*" brings about a considerable transfer of meaning: "Islam *in* France" means that Islam is a foreign body in French society; "Islam *of* France" identifies that Islam is now a part of French identity, it is in its own home. This is, in fact, a wide and favourable interpretation of Pasqua's formula. A closer reading however, could lead us to understand it quite differently: "Islam *of* France" could mean, by a slight extension, that the French Muslims have to produce an "adapted Islam", a "French Islam", in accordance with their new environment and, so, stop referring to the notion of "*Sharīʿa*" or wearing the scarf or anything else that could be "too visible".

15. One of the most important deficiencies in a majority of studies today is the fact that their authors, the new "specialists of contemporary Islam" in Western universities, are almost exclusively formed in the Social Sciences. They often have no idea about theological references linked with a religious way of life. According to them, religions are "matter-of-fact" produced and are, at once, the agents of social dynamics and their historical evolution. This posture could, of course, be academically legitimated. Nevertheless, it is simplistic and does not render all aspects of the question of the Muslim presence, not only as Believers but also as practising, in a secular society.

16. This fact, so evident, should have immediate implications for Muslims' discourses and behaviours but, unfortunately, it falls far short of this.

17. *Ḥadīth* (Bukhārī and Muslim).

18. We have to mention, nevertheless, that the state of education in French suburbs is nowadays catastrophic: insalubrious buildings, on-going violence and delinquency make teaching almost impossible for a frightened staff. In the suburbs, the majority of the latter are not volunteers: the teaching system in France does not give teachers, at least the new ones, the choice of school in which they work. Second and third immigrant generations are the principal victims of this state of affairs.

19. The question of visibility is crucial: between 4 and 5 million Muslims live in France today. Even if less than 15% practise their religion every day, their visibility is important and provokes doubts and tensions in the average French population. The words which are commonly used by people in surveys about

28

immigration, foreigners and Islam are "invasion", "strange", "not-from-here". Islam is always perceived as a "foreign religion" or "the religion of foreigners" and, in this sense, the idea of "invasion" reveals, among other things, the hidden French fear of losing both references and cultural identity.

20. The different estimates are contradictory. If we rely on what the Muslims say of their own practise, the rate increases to about 31% (see Questionnaire on Prayer, p. 47) but this figure does not match reality.

21. We will discuss this question a little later on.

22. Jørgen Nielsen, *Muslims in Western Europe*, 2nd Edition (Edinburgh University Press, 1995), p. 13.

23. Ibid.

24. This is the figure advanced by Moustapha Diop and quoted by Abou Diab Khattar in a recent article published by the magazine *Arabies,* Paris (October 1996), p.14. It confirms figures presented in many other researches.

25. See *Arabies*, Paris (October 1996), pp. 17–20.

26. In spite of all its deficiencies, the independence of the judicial power is more effective in Western countries than in any Muslim ones. In the latter, the degree of corruption is so high and the link between juridical power and the political is so obscure that it is impossible to trust legal decisions. The recent "affairs" in many Western countries (United States, France, Spain, Italy for example) reveal that corruption is now deeply spread in the judiciary. This is also a fact but it concerns some important strategic matters (trade unions, elections, financial commitments and so forth): however, this scarcely concerns the rights of individuals or associations either at local or national level.

27. In a recent case, in Nancy (13th September 1995), the Administrative Courts even decided that the young Muslim girl had to be compensated for the trouble caused by the illegal decision to expel her.

28. One cannot ignore another kind of fear which concerns what happens in South Mediterranean countries, and especially in Algeria. The historical (and colonialist) relations between France and Algeria still dwell in the French authorities' minds. There are, all the more so, new stakes in Algeria today and the French government is clearly implicated and supports Zerual's regime. At the same time, it exerts pressure and constantly watches over Muslim associations and groups. Police interventions are very frequent and treatments inflicted, in the police station, on youths arrested are sometimes humiliating and degrading (abuses, insults, physical blows, cigarettes stubbed out on the arms and so forth). In one police station near Lyon young Muslims were constrained to watch a pornographic film to prove that they were not "pure" Islamists. International involvement leads the French government to manage Islamic affairs as if it only concerns the police or terrorist squads. Many political or religious personalities, such as the well-known priest Christian Delorme, have asked the government to change this policy which has many negative effects on young Muslim generations and which will leave deep and irreparable scars in the future.

29. With this concept (*"insertion"* in French) they mean a "community integration" and it refers, in contrast, to the "multiculturalism" of the Anglo-Saxon model.

30. Many French scholars, including the anthropologist Edgard Morin and the scholar Dominique Wolton, are contesting the principle of a restrictive, and so very dangerous, "Economic Community". In the name of economic interests, social questions and regional customs are knowingly neglected to build one European standard model of behaviour and taste, polished and purified from every provincial particularism (tradition, culture, language, etc.). According to these scholars, we are not witnessing the European community's birth but its death from its own roots.

31. See for example, Bruno Etienne, *L'islam en France* (Editions du CNRS, Paris, 1990); Gilles Kepel, *Les Banlieues de l'Islam* (Editions du Seuil, Paris, 1987) and *A l'Ouest d'Allah* (Editions du Seuil, Paris, 1994).

32. The Agreement between the Spanish Government and the Muslim Committee (1992) is of a completely different nature (see the complete text of this Agreement in *Encounters: Journal of Inter-Cultural Perspectives*, Islamic Foundation, Leicester, 2:2 (September 1996).

33. Jocelyn Cesari, *Etre Musulman en France* (Karthala, Paris, 1994), pp. 147–56.

34. See Tariq Ramadan, "Pour un Nouveau Cadre Laïque" in *L'Evénement Estudiantin*, revue de l'UISEF (Islamic Union of Muslim Students in France), No. 5 (1995) and "Pour une Laïcité Ouverte (To an Open Secularism)" in *Le Monde* (13th October 1994).

PART II

The Way Forward

A. A Question of Representation

During the first 30 years of the new[1] Islamic presence in France, Muslim North African and Turkish workers were often very discreet concerning their religion and their identity. They were in France for work and for the most part they felt that they were not at home: one day, they would return to where they had come from, to their own country. What occurred in France was clearly not their concern: they were pushed by economic interests, this was not only their priority but the only target of their migration far from their own families and roots. Their modest background and their immediate survival priorities dictated that, during the first period of migration, they did not think about what shape the Muslim presence in France would take. They always thought of going back home one day, so the question of staying never occurred to them.

However, as time passed, children were born and raised in France and it became impossible for the first generation of migrant Muslims to easily envisage going back to their country of origin. Furthermore, the children of second generation Muslims are French. The parents are perhaps foreigners but not their children. Additionally, the generation gap between the two widened over the years, the parents retaining their nostalgia of the past and their birthplace. Their children's minds could not grasp such sentiments for the horizon of their memories stopped at the boundaries of the neighbourhood or the city in which they had been brought up and in which they had always lived. Their own growing up did not mirror their parents' past and a break developed between the generations. This in itself was a period of crisis during which the Muslims had for the first time to think about the reality of being French Muslims.

Muslim organisations had been active in France for a long time, particularly a group of students around Professor Muhammad Hamidullah who were to found the Association of Muslim Students in France (*Association des Musulmans Islamiques de France*) in 1963; his Islamic Cultural Centre, however, had been active since 1956. Their activities, of great importance and considerable impact, were essentially directed towards students and academic circles and did not reach the general immigrant populace. Other organisations did work locally but those actions, even taken together, did not have any significant impact at grass roots level.[2]

The deep social crisis, at the beginning of the 1970s, changed the face of the situation. The youth, whose parents were originally from Algeria, Morocco or Tunisia, often lived in insalubrious neighbourhoods or suburbs neglected and ignored by political leaders. They found neither their identity nor their place in this social climate recognised and began to ask, as French Muslims, for their rights, such a thing which the first generation had never dared to do. This break between the generations was very significant and it was first visible during the late 1970s and early 1980s.

Some of the young Muslims of the second and third generations joined associations or cultural movements, especially during the mid 1980s, not least the *SOS Racism* organisation, which was considerably popularised through the media (and via the strong personality of its President, Harlem Désir). At the same time, a new Islamic consciousness was gathering pace in many French cities such as Paris, Lyon, Marseille and Grenoble. Many youth were not only searching for their identity but were also determined to claim that their identity demands respect. In the meantime, the October 1981 Act which had allowed for the creation of associations, resulted in the growth of Muslim organisations both at local and national levels. During the 1980s, these Islamic organisations diversified their activities and the problem of representation inevitably provoked tension among the Muslims. New, important, national organisations were born in this decade, such as the Union of Islamic Organisations in France (*Union des Organisations Islamiques de France*, UOIF, Paris, 1983), the National Federation of Muslims in France (*Fédération Nationale des Musulmans de France*, FNMF, Paris, 1985), the Union of Young

Muslims (*Union des Jeunes Musulmans*, UJM, Lyon, 1987) and the Young Muslims of France (*Jeunes Musulmans de France*, JMF, Paris, 1992). The French State – which had been in constant contact with the Paris Mosque as a natural consequence of its relations with the Algerian government – decided to intervene in a clear manner and set up, in 1990, under the socialist regime, the CORIF (*Conseil de Réflexion sur l'Islam en France*), Council of Reflection on Islam in France, a think tank for Islam in France. This was a consultative council created by the Home Minister, Pierre Joxe, and headed by a member of his department. Thus, the government managed to master the problem by creating a platform of "representation" for Muslims. This intervention was to be much criticised and had neither any impact on nor any recognition from the Muslim community in France. Charles Pasqua, the Home Minister's successor during the so-called "*cohabitation*"[3] in the French regime (1993–95) neglected CORIF, preferring a direct and personal intervention in Islamic affairs by choosing his broker (beginning with Dalil Boubakeur, Rector of the Paris Mosque). Nevertheless, the situation did not tangibly improve and the creation of an independent National Muslim Coordination Council in 1993 and, afterwards, of the Consultative Council of Muslims of France in 1995 – guided by the Paris Mosque with the backing of the French government[4] – did not have any impact either.

The last attempt to structure the Muslims in France, in December 1995, with the High Council of Muslims in France was nearly stillborn. Headed by two of Chirac's partisans (Ms. Khadija Khali and Mrs. Abderrahmane Dahmane), the committee split in two after only a few months and actually has no contact with Muslims at the grass roots. For private reasons, all its actions are oriented against the Paris Mosque in order to fight it for official representation: the Muslims, as a whole, however, are very far removed from these disputes and strategies and do not recognise themselves in a struggle which implies men and women seemingly fond of power alone.

Nowadays there is no structure which genuinely represents Muslims. Approximately 1,400 organisations exist today in France. Some are involved in a federate structure (the UOIF, the most important, has 200–250 associations affiliated to it or the FNMF, with between 50 and 70, the AEIF, the JMF, the Network of Young Muslims of France – based mainly around the UJM – the *Jamā ʿat at-Tablīgh* or the Paris Mosque, are all linked with local affiliates or groups), but activities are dispersed and chaos seems to reign. At local level, Muslims appear preoccupied with other problems and a majority of associations try to find solutions in order to protect and affirm their Muslim identity.

B. Within the Muslim Community

We have related above the kinds of problems which the Muslim community faced during the first and almost the whole of the second decade of their presence in France. Those early days were very difficult and, as a natural consequence, the Muslims who arrived at this time from their country of origin first thought to protect their identity and their religion in this new and foreign environment. They went to work and never thought to ask anything from the land which provided them with that opportunity. Little by little, with the growth of these Muslim immigrants in the workplace, facilities were provided for them to pray. This process continued almost unnoticed and French members of trade unions who defended their workmates and struggled for "the rights of immigrant workers" were perhaps not aware of the religious or cultural implications of their support. It appeared normal and fair to respect the faith of other "workers", *a fortiori* when these practices were very discreet.

Those first immigrants used to be reserved and unassuming, learning to withdraw into themselves. When they were allowed to bring their wives and children to France, their attitude regarding their relatives remained the same: they taught them to be discreet and cautious as well. They were not at home and the only thing they could do was protect themselves, and certainly not disturb the rules and norms of their host society. This was also the attitude of a majority of Islamic scholars who thought that Muslims had to be careful and not involve themselves in the social or political affairs of the country but simply preserve their Muslim identity and so not dilute themselves into this foreign, Western country. The Muslims should avoid too intimate and prolonged contacts with the indigenous people and the first mosques were thought of not only as mere places of worship, but also as refuges from an insidious cultural invasion liable to imbue immigrants' minds and hearts.

Many *'ulamā'* emphasised, until the beginning of the 1980s, that Muslims should not take up French nationality even if there were such facilities for children born in France.[5] They encouraged the immigrants of the first generation to preserve a strong link with their country of origin, its language and sometimes its government. In the mosques, with very few exceptions, lectures, speeches and sermons were given in Arabic. It was as if the Muslims created a culture within a culture, a small protected island or, more precisely, a pocket of resistance against an environment perceived as hazardous and treacherous. These then were the warning signs of an increasing crisis of identity.

The presence and attitude of the children of the second and third generations was to bring this posture back into question. At least two clear messages were conveyed. First, it became clear that any *return* would not take place and that the idea of "going back home" was for the majority of Muslims, nothing but a myth. Second, the children knew and in fact, had, no land but France and the initial attitude of their parents to try to keep them close to themselves, protecting them against this hostile environment, had had a totally opposite effect to what they expected. As a result, the defensive and reactive posture of the first generation, instead of preserving the *original* identity of their children, widened the gap between parents and offspring. Slowly, but very deeply, French culture and habits had taken *possession* of the children.

The young generation were French, whether their parents liked it or not; they were French and they were Muslim. This, in itself, did not solve any problems but, on the contrary, created a new, more complex and intricate difficulty which was to be met with by all Muslim organisations in the future: the question was not only "how to be Muslim in France" but "how to be Muslim and French". The former situation could have left a slight margin for the uprooted mentality and its consequences; the latter, however, did not facilitate this.

Awareness of this substantial shift occurred during the second half of the 1980s. In different cities, many organisations came to modify their approach, influenced as they were by the example of a new kind of involvement from the youth of the second generation. Lectures about Islam, courses, training and even Friday sermons began to be given in French. Furthermore, the number of meetings, conferences and general activities increased considerably. In cities such as Lille, Bordeaux, Lyon, Paris, Marseille and Strasbourg, Muslim organisations have begun to provide community assistance for Muslims in various fields: tutorial classes, cultural activities, sports, trips, and the like. Several attempts regarding the taking charge of and helping drug addicts took place with more or less success but this represented evidence, one among many others, that Muslims had developed a deep consciousness of their new responsibility within French society and were ready to be involved in and compete with others.

Gradually, the meetings and activities have become much more frequent and it is not uncommon for 500, 800 or 1,000 people to attend an Islamic lecture. The annual meeting of the UOIF, in Paris in December 1995, gathered together about 30,000 Muslims (recognised as the most important annual assembly of Muslims anywhere in Europe). The presence of young Muslims throughout France at different levels (their activities in the suburbs as well as in the universities have also significantly increased over the last five years) and their claims to have more mosques, *halāl* food and official recognition – at local level – have refined the problems of the Muslims in France. The parents of the first generation, still close mentally to their roots, were almost "invisible" in France, whereas their children, living in "their" country, have become more "visible" and with a much clearer consciousness of the duties of their religion. Seemingly paradoxical, this process is nevertheless completely natural: after the understandable reactive posture of the first immigrants, the self-assertion of the youth is quite normal, this coupled with the fact of their asking for a recognition of their religion not least by rediscovering it as a part of their own identity.

This recognition, which is evident in the demand for mosques (or offices) and a more significant visibility within French society (in particular, the scarf worn by young Muslim girls), could have led to one of the most important misunderstandings between the real intentions of the Muslims and the immediate perception and comprehension of such claims by the indigenous French. Jocelyn Cesari aptly explains that the Muslims' demand for mosques, their specific diet and cemetery requirements, all of which should have been seen as signs of "integration" – the Muslims expressing in this way the fact that they are here to stay, that they are at home and, as a natural consequence, that they expect *their* society to provide them with all that they need to achieve their religious duties and so live in harmony with their intimate creed – have been totally misunderstood and erroneously analysed.[6] Many sociologists and, following in their footsteps, the French population, have thought it a clear and obvious sign of a refusal of "integration" and, more widely, of French values and their republican traditions. For the Muslims, it represented a manifest acceptance of the fact ("we are Muslims and French"); whereas for the French population it appeared to be a colonising and sweeping into society motivated by hazy intentions and an ulterior motive of proselytism – known to be the essence of the Muslim attitude.

This was, effectively, a period of crisis between the end of the 1980s and the beginning of the 1990s during which the new dynamics that occurred in Muslim organisations were very badly received by the French population. Two main factors were to accentuate this fracture: first, the incapacity of Muslim leaders to convey and clearly explain what they wanted and their inability to develop a broad scale of relations with different authorities within French society (local authorities, social workers, scholars, journalists, political parties, and the like); second, the situation in Algeria has interfered in the state of Muslim affairs in France. Since 1988, each violent event which has hit Algerian society (the first riots in 1988, the growth of the FIS and, finally, since 1991, the so-called Civil War with its dreadful violence) has had effects both on popular sentiment and internal political decisions.[7]

The pressure on Muslims in France remains very strong and the strained atmosphere hides and reveals many mutual suspicions. Nevertheless, things have moved and evolved in many sectors: for instance, as we have pointed out earlier, a majority of the Administrative Courts issued decisions in favour of the young Muslim girls concerning their right to wear scarves at school. Many institutions, pro-secular by tradition, such as *La Ligue de l'Enseignement* ("The Teaching League"), the French League of Human Rights and the well-known academic magazine *L'Esprit* ("The Mind") are now interested in engaging in a thorough dialogue with Muslim organisations.

Furthermore, in November 1996, a regional branch of the French Socialist Party, organised, in Reims, an important meeting regarding the question of secularism in France. This was in response to the Pope's visit to the city to celebrate the anniversary of Clovis's conversion to Christianity. It was clear, then, that the problem of secularism is not just linked with the question of Islam and the mere visit of the Pope (September 1996) provoked intense reactions among groups which argued that French secular authorities have nothing to do with such a *religious* anniversary, even, and above all, if it is said to represent the symbol of the birth of "Catholic France".[8] During the meeting, the question of Islam arose in a specific round table discussion and it appeared that a majority of the participants (politicians, journalists, social workers, etc.) were ready to hear and even support the Muslim claim for a respect of their identity within the French Constitutional framework; a framework which, in fact, offers them almost complete freedom to practise their religion.[9]

Such official – and unofficial – initiatives and encounters have multiplied during the last five years, paradoxically generated by the tense atmosphere relating to the question of Islam and the State in France. Today, many Muslims and Muslim organisations are involved, at different levels, in a fruitful and engaging dialogue with the players in the French social system. Many of the latter have understood that it is not possible to build a future based on peace and mutual respect by ignoring the longings of young generations for a true recognition of their Muslim identity. It seems they have understood that the *official* Muslim leaders – almost exclusively recognised as such by the authorities – have neither the trust of the majority of Muslims nor a real involvement at grass roots level. Therefore, in recent years, one has witnessed a new dynamic within the Muslim collective life in France. It is most unlikely to solve the manifold and complicated problems of identity, schools, or representation discussed above but it is clear that this new kind of commitment is to help Muslims become more deeply established in French society so as to be a real part, a genuine component, of it, both in its social and political aspects.

Notes

1. The Muslim presence in France does, in fact, date back to the 8th century and many researchers forget that Islam also partakes of French culture and civilisation. The current presence is due to immigration after the First World War; it is of a *new* kind but is not the first.

2. The French section of *Jamāʿat at-Tablīgh* was founded in 1968 but its actions became more visible at the end of the 1970s.

3. The President, François Mitterand, represented the Socialist Party while the Prime Minister, Jacques Chirac, was from the right wing party, the RPR (Rassemblement pour la République).

4. This Consultative Council published a *Charter of Islam in France,* the text of which attempts to organise Islam in France from the appointment of *Imāms*, the running of Mosques to the control of *ḥalāl* food (the French government had given to the Paris Mosque almost a complete monopoly on the management of *ḥalāl* meat in France). This Charter did not have any real impact, especially after the Presidential election in May 1996 and the victory of Jacques Chirac. Dalil Boubakeur miscalculated sympathies in the election, choosing to support his rival, the former Prime Minister Jacques Balladur. In February 1996, the government decided to withdraw its support from the Paris Mosque, its official delegation not attending (as it did in previous years) the official ceremony marking the end of Ramaḍān.

5. According to French law a child born in France has the right to be French.

6. See her interesting analysis in *Etre Musulman en France* (Karthala, Paris, 1994).

7. The bomb attacks in Paris during the Summer of 1995 and in December 1996, have had a significant impact on French society and have increased the tendency to confuse Islam and terrorism in the minds of many people. In a recent survey about "terrorism", 87% of the French students polled linked Islam with *"intégrisme"* and terrorism. See *Sondage pour le Colloque du Memorial de Caen, De la Religion à la l'Intégrisme, de la Paix à la Guerre* (From Religion to Fundamentalism, from Peace to War), November 1996.

8. There were many similar reactions following the death of the former President François Mitterand, because of the *national* mass celebrated in the presence of the current President. Strict secular partisans argued that the French State is secular and, thus, has to be neutral even regarding the death of its President. According to them, this religious ceremony was a private affair and did not have to be so *public.*

9. Many of the participants clearly said that the scarf in school was not contrary to the principle of secularism and that it has to be respected but the clauses of the "tacit contract" with the Muslim girls have to be clear: neither proselytism nor absence from certain courses (biology or physical education) could be accepted. In view of this, the most radical opponents to the wearing of the scarf at school seem to have modified their strategy. Some teachers refuse henceforth to teach their courses if veiled girls are present in the class. Encouraging what they call a "legitimate resistance", a few scholars, such as Guy Coq, asked for a change in the law especially as regards "the specific conditions of secularism within school". See the magazine *L'Express*, "Voile, La Faute au Conseil d'Etat" ("Scarf, the Fault of the State Council"), (5th December 1996), p. 30. This was the first time that this kind of claim appeared in the debate regarding Islam; hitherto, Muslims were suspected – and reproached – for attempting to modify the law and, thus, of bringing back into question the French secular identity. Becoming aware that Muslim claims fit the framework not only of the French Constitution (the multiplicity of Court decisions in favour of the Muslim girls reinforces this assertion) but also the clauses of the European Convention of Human Rights, these academics try to shift the debate in a "new" direction. It is they, this time, who ask for new legislation (less *lax* than the current one) to protect both the rights of women and the specific identity of the French Republic. See the newspaper *Libération* (8th November 1996), expressing this view, "Les Voiles et la République" ("The Scarves and the Republic") by Guy Coq. One notices that the "*Islamic* scarves" are henceforth called "*Islamist* scarves" and this, in itself, has a political connotation.

Conclusion

A new religious and political awareness has been growing among the Muslims during the last ten years, especially amongst the young generations. A creative approach is evident in this respect, one which associates with the need to affirm and protect religious identity and, at the same time, to build bridges with the indigenous population by engaging more in the social and the political life of society at large. The huge and successful campaign (1994–95) conducted by the Network of Young Muslims in France, appealing to young French Muslims to vote and try to constitute a group of "100,000" Muslim voters, is clear evidence of this dynamic role. Less linked to their countries of origin (and their governments) than their previous generations, these young Muslims have given rise to a new kind of posture which could give birth to a genuine French Muslim identity. The young Muslim generation, between 25 and 35 years of age, are exhausting themselves trying to find a way to achieve their aim, an aim which requires a delicate balance between the protection of their Muslim identity and the danger of involvement in a non-Muslim society.

Things, however, are not so simple as we have discussed in this study and the French Muslim community is facing profound challenges which hinder its progress. After more than 30 years of confinement and ten years of assessment and reorientation, the reality remains harsh: 84% of Muslims do not practise their religion, an increasing number of them are affected by delinquency, drug addiction and marginalisation. Between 25 and 30% of prisoners in France are of North African origin. These figures speak for themselves and bring to the fore the urgent necessity to provide an Islamic education and consciousness for a reassessment of the situation.

In fact, the question of education in general and of an Islamic education in particular, like anywhere in Europe, remains one of the most important preoccupations of the Islamic community in France. We are not just talking here of a traditional form of religious education but also the wider concept of a general Islamic education appropriate to a European context. A few Muslim scholars living in France have tried, during the last three years, to engage in reflection on this topic[1] but their works are largely unknown or untested. The idea of founding Islamic schools is spreading among Muslims and this represents the hope for the future. Indeed, this remains an *attractive* idea but requires a kind of passivity among Muslims not only to re-think their way but also to re-think the content of Islamic education currently taught with a view to providing a serious and global extra-curricular Islamic teaching. This is the only way to face up to the needs of millions of young Muslims of the second, third and fourth generations whose majority cannot be integrated with the dreamed-of Islamic structure.

For the time being, however, many new traditionalist or radical movements[2] continue to appear and these do not facilitate positive and constructive thought and action. On the contrary, they emphasise division and sometimes paralyse Islamic activities in a whole city. The young, whose parents are Muslims from North Africa, and who live in poor suburbs are attracted to these kinds of groups. By proposing a rupture with French society they respond to the natural inclination of these youth who determine their identity *against* France and its social structures which have marginalised them during the last two decades. Their Islamic identity is understood as an identity of protest, reaction, and refusal and this makes it difficult to deal with them as they claim to refuse a "soft and compromised Islam". The fact that such groups are growing in the suburbs demands our urgent attention, not least in developing educational and social action at grass roots levels. The French State seems overtaken by the extent of this task and, as we have stated earlier, continues to approach with suspicion all Islamic organisations even when they are involved in social welfare activities. They suspect that their undeclared objective is proselytism hidden behind a mask of social welfare. Nevertheless, if Muslim organisations wish to prevent irreversible damage within their community, they must provide both education and social support to families and individuals especially when a large number of them emanate from poor backgrounds.

The situation also requires that Muslims establish links with the social and political actors of French society both at the local and national level. Many youth associations are already engaged in this process and a large number of meetings are organised throughout France on different subjects, such as secularism, modernity, health, faith, dialogue, reciprocity, social problems, and the like. This is a sign that things are progressing and that the new generations are more aware than their parents of the necessity to promote a comprehensive and sustained religious, cultural and even social dialogue within French society from the moment they consider themselves a part of this society.

In this respect, the question of representation, though it is important, is not a priority. Its permanent appearance in the debate, concerning Islam, provokes divisions and hinders its progress. Indeed, it is not the main problem for the youth who, today, have other, more specific problems and preoccupations. The youth should urge the leaders of the Muslim community to reset their priorities within the purview of their activities. They should at least begin to work together to face up to the deeper problems the community has today and that no representation of any kind would be able to solve by its mere presence, however competent and dedicated it may be. Far from the French State and the stake of official recognition, Muslims in France have to show their capacity to decide what kind of presence they want. In so doing, they should reorient their activities towards their own community and redirect them according to the context which requires, at this time of crisis, both an internal project of global education (religious, social and political) and an external involvement in every sphere of activity within French society which is, from this time on, theirs.

Notes

1. They are globally at one with the reflection already spread in the UK (see Khurram Murad's works, for instance, *Muslim Youth in the West: Towards a New Education Strategy* (Islamic Foundation, Leicester, 1986) or in Germany, Austria and the United States.

2. The "*Ahbach*" tendency supported by the Syrian government and whose headquarters is in Lebanon now has several mosques in France (Montpellier, Paris, Lyon, etc.). It is a traditionalist group, which fights all "Islamists" whom they label as "radical fundamentalists". They describe themselves as moderate, refusing to be involved in any political debate. In the religious field, they concentrate on specific issues such as *Tawḥīd, al-asmā' wa aṣ-Ṣifāt* (God's names and attributes), life in the Hereafter (Hell and Heaven) and assert, for instance, that Ibn Taymiyya, Ḥasan al-Banna, Muḥammad al-Ghazālī and Yūsuf al-Qarḍāwī hold positions that lead to *kufr* (by denying the truth). Many other so-called *salafī* groups – influenced by the Wahhābī school of thought – are active in France and find their echo within a youth desirous of not engaging in any kind of relations with French society "which are not Islamic" (this is often a very reactive attitude). At the same time, political groups, particularly radical ones, have appeared in France after the electoral process in Algeria was stopped in December 1991, as well as branches of the Liberation Party (*Ḥizb at-Taḥrīr*) claiming restoration of the Caliphate.

Appendix

Muslims in France by Origin (official figures)

Algeria	614,207
Morocco	572,652
Tunisia	206,336
Turkey	197,712
Senegal	43,044
Mali	37,693
Lebanon	20,953

Based on: "Recensement INSEE 1990" – in *La Connaissance de l'Immigration et de l'Integration*, Decembre 1992. (Rapport au Premier Ministre, La Documentation Francaise, Decembre 1992) p.96.

Questionnaire on Prayer

Question: Do you pray every day?

	Number of Muslims	
	1994 (%)	1989 (%)
Yes	31	41
No	69	59
No Comment	–	–
TOTAL	100	100

Based on: Sondage IFOP, 1994

Question: Do you go to the mosque on Friday?

	Number of Muslims	
	1994 (%)	1989 (%)
Yes	16	16
No	84	83
No Comment	–	1
TOTAL	100	100

Based on: Sondage IFOP, 1994

Mixed Marriages According to the Nationality of the Foreigner, Between 1981 and 1992

Nationality	Number of Mixed Marriages		Gender of French Spouse for 1992 Figures	
	1981	1992	French Male	French Female
Algerian	2,568	5,726	2,343	3,383
Moroccan	1,101	5,015	1,883	3,182
Tunisian	747	1,309	223	1,086

Based on: A. Nyer Malbet, *Migrations et Conditions Sanitaires*, (L'Harmattan, 1995).

Marriages Between North African
Women and French Men

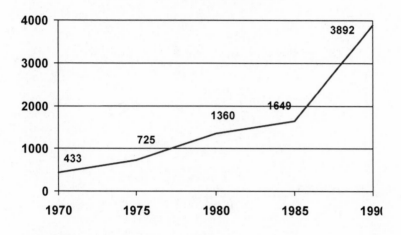

Source: P. Bernard, *L'immigration* (Le Monde Poche, 1993) p.98. This figure is based on Ministere des Affaires Sociales.

Bibliography

Books

Baubérot, Jean, *La Laïcité, quel Héritage?* (Labor et Fides, Paris, 1990).

Cesari, Jocelyn, *Etre Musulman en France* (Karthala, Paris, 1994).

Consultative Council, Mosque of Paris, *Charter of Islam in France* (Mosque of Paris, January 1995).

Etienne, Bruno, *L'islam en France* (Editions du CNRS, Paris, 1990).

Kepel, Gilles, *A l'Ouest d'Allah* (Editions du Seuil, Paris, 1994). (English translation: *Allah in the West, Islamic Movements in America and Europe*, Polity Press, London, 1997.)

———, *Les Banlieues de l'Islam, Naissance d'une Religion en France* (Editions du Seuil, Paris, 1987).

Morsy, Magali, *Demain, L'Islam de France* (MAME, Paris, 1993).

Murad, Khurram, *Muslim Youth in the West: Towards a New Education Strategy* (Islamic Foundation, Leicester, 1986).

Nielsen, Jørgen, *Muslims in Western Europe*, 2nd Ed., Islamic Surveys. (Edinburgh University Press, 1995).

Ramadan, Tariq, *Les Musulmans dans la Laïcité* (Tawḥīd, Lyon, 1994), 2nd Ed., 1998.

Shadid, W.A.R. and Koningsveld, P.S. Van (eds.), *Muslims in the Margin: Political Responses to the Presence of Islam in Western Europe* (Pharos, Den Haag, 1996).

Articles

Ballard, Roger, "Islam and the Construction of Europe", in *Muslims in the Margin: Political Responses to the Presence of Islam in Western Europe* (Pharos, Den Haag, 1996).

Colloque de Caen, "Sondage pour le Colloque du Memorial de Caen, De la Religion à la l'Intégrisme, de la Paix à la Guerre" ("From Religion to Fundamentalism, from Peace to War"), November 1996.

Coq, Guy, "Les Voiles et la République" ("The Scarves and the Republic"), in *Libération* (8th November 1996).

——, "Voile, La Faute au Conseil" ("Scarf, the Fault of the State Council"), in *L'Express* (5th December 1996).

Khattar, Abou Diab, *Arabies* (magazine), Paris (October 1996).

Ramadan, Tariq, "Pour un Nouveau Cadre Laïque", in *L'Evénement Estudiantin*, revue de l'UISEF, No. 5 (1995).

——, "Pour une Laïcité Ouverte", in *Le Monde* (13th October 1994).

——, "Islam de France, Etat des Lieux et Perspectives", in *Les Idees en Mouvement*, Journal de la Ligue Francaise de l'Enseignement (April 1998).

Viorst, Milton, "The Muslims of France", in *Foreign Affairs,* Washington, DC (September/October 1996).

Withol de Wenden, Catherine, "Muslims in France", in *Muslims in the Margin: Political Responses to the Presence of Islam in Western Europe* (Pharos, Den Haag, 1996).

Index

53